ARTIST TRANSCRIPTIONS TROMBONE

THE Steve Turre COLLECTION

Transcriptions by Steve Turre and John Farnsworth

ISBN 978-0-634-03142-7

HAL•LEONARD® CORPORATION

7777 W. BLUEMOUND RD. P.O. BOX 13819 MILWAUKEE, WI 53213

Visit Hal Leonard Online at
www.halleonard.com

BIOGRAPHY

One of the world's preeminent jazz innovators, trombonist and seashellist Steve Turre has consistently won both the Readers' and Critics' polls in *JazzTimes, DownBeat,* and *Jazziz* for Best Trombone and for Best Miscellaneous Instrumentalist (shells). Turre was born to Mexican-American parents and grew up in the San Francisco Bay area where he absorbed daily doses of mariachi, blues and jazz. While attending Sacramento State University, he joined the Escovedo Brothers salsa band, which began his career-long involvement with that genre.

In 1972 Steve Turre's career picked up momentum when Ray Charles hired him to go on tour. A year later, Turre's mentor Woody Shaw brought him into Art Blakey's Jazz Messengers. After his tenure with Blakey, Turre went on to work with a diverse list of musicians from the jazz, Latin, and pop worlds, including Dizzy Gillespie, McCoy Tyner, J.J. Johnson, Herbie Hancock, Lester Bowie, Tito Puente, Mongo Santamaria, Van Morrison, Pharoah Sanders, Horace Silver, Max Roach, and Rahsaan Roland Kirk. The latter introduced him to the seashell as an instrument. Soon thereafter, while Steve was touring in Mexico City with Woody Shaw, his relatives informed him that his ancestors had played the shells. Since then, Turre has incorporated seashells into his diverse musical style.

In addition to performing as a member of the Saturday Night Live Band since 1984, Turre leads several different ensembles. Sanctified Shells utilizes the seashell in a larger context, transforming his horn section into a "shell choir." Turre's spring of 1999 Verve release, *Lotus Flower*, showcases his Sextet With Strings. The recording explores many great standards and original compositions arranged by Turre for the unique instrumentation of trombone and shells, violin, cello, piano, bass and drums. Turre's quartet and quintet provide a setting based in tradition, while stretching the limits conceptually and stylistically. In the summer of 2000, Telarc released *In the Spur of the Moment*. This recording features Steve with three different quartets, each with a different and distinct master pianist: Ray Charles, Chucho Valdes, and Stephen Scott.

Turre's self-titled Verve release pioneers a unique artistic vision, drawing upon jazz, Afro-Cuban, and Brazilian sources. This innovative recording also features Cassandra Wilson, Randy Brecker, Graciela, Mongo Santamaria and J.J. Johnson. Previously, Turre recorded *Right There* and *Rhythm Within*, featuring Herbie Hancock, Jon Faddis, Pharoah Sanders; and *Sanctified Shells*, on Verve's subsidiary label, Antilles.

Steve Turre continually evolves as a musician and arranger. He has a strong command of all musical genres, and when it comes to his distinct brand of jazz, he always keeps one foot in the past and one in the future.

DISCOGRAPHY

Blackfoot – *Lotus Flower* (Verve 314 559 787-2)
Body and Soul – *Rhythm Within* (Antilles 314 527 159-2)
Echoes of Harlem – *Right There* (Antilles 314 510 040-2)
In a Sentimental Mood – *Viewpoints and Vibrations* (Stash ST-CD-2)
Lament – *Viewpoints and Vibrations* (Stash ST-CD-2)
Let It Go – *Steve Turre* (Verve 314 537 133-2)
Misty – *In the Spur of the Moment* (Telarc 83484)
Mood Indigo – *Fire and Ice* (Stash ST-CD-7)
The Nearness of You – *TNT* (Telarc 83529)
Puente of Soul – *TNT* (Telarc 83529)
Ray's Collard Greens – *In the Spur of the Moment* (Telarc 83484)
Something for John – *In the Spur of the Moment* (Telarc 83484)
Stompin' at the Savoy – *TNT* (Telarc 83529)
You Are the Sunshine of My Life – *Fire and Ice* (Stash ST-CD-7)

PREFACE

This book has been a long time coming, and it was for the simple reason that I wanted it to be right! Having struggled with various interpretations of my work, I decided to do it myself with the help of my good friend John Farnsworth. It took countless hours, but I decided to re-learn my solos and write down what I actually played, including all alternate positions, articulations and complete plunger notations.

Much to my surprise, it was quite difficult to play my own solos! They were created spontaneously, "in the moment," and to recapture that energy and feeling required quite a bit of repetition and deep listening for nuance. For the same reason, I suggest that you get the recordings — so you can not only see the music, but hear it too!

After I learned to play my solos, it was necessary to write down exactly what was performed. That's where John Farnsworth's fabulous ears came into play. As you may know, there can be multiple ways to write the same thing, and for John and myself, the challenge was to find the best way to write the music out, especially the rhythms. Sometimes the commonly accepted way to write jazz rhythms, assuming that eighth notes are "swung," is not the way they are really articulated. To me, articulation is very, very important, not only for rhythm, but for nuance, too. Sometimes, rhythms fall "in the cracks," and although they sound quite natural when you hear them, when you go to write them out, it can give you fits! There is one four-

Steve, with John Farnsworth

bar phrase of "Stompin' at the Savoy" (during the second trombone entrance, after the bridge, on the "trades" with the brushes/drums) on which we must have spent eight hours! I feel it's still an approximation, but if you "stretch the time" a little, it will lay in the pocket. That's how our music is — the feeling comes first! We felt that it is better to write "LAY BACK," than to try to approximate something with sixty-fourth rests and weird notations that end up being guessed at anyway.

Considering all the detail involved, we made a real effort to make everything in this book as clear and easy to read as possible. The plunger transcriptions were especially challenging! I want to give my heart felt thanks to John Farnsworth for all his expertise, because this book would not have been the same without his help.

Preparing this book has been a real learning experience for me. As the years go by, my playing has evolved and I don't play exactly the same things I used to play in the '80s — and some of these solos are from my first recordings. I'm hearing differently now, but I still draw upon my foundation. This project has given me renewed inspiration to keep drawing on that foundation, and the foundation of those that came before me. Remember, as far back as you can go will directly influence how far forward you will go!

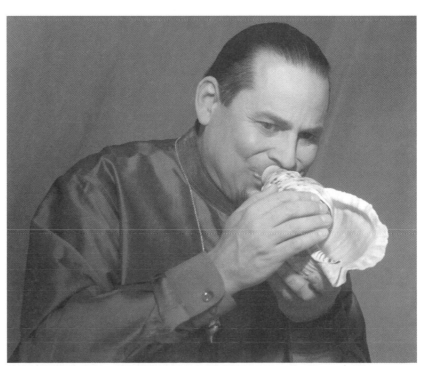

Enjoy,

Steve Turre

Blackfoot

By Steve Turre

Blackfoot

Blackfoot

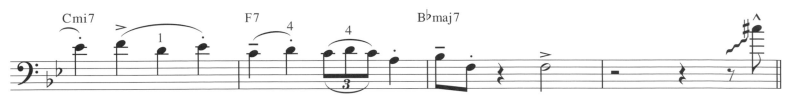

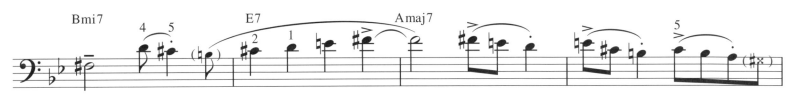

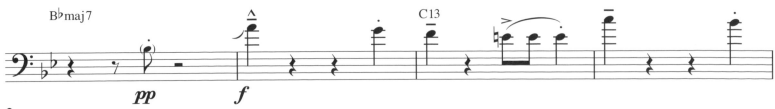

Blackfoot

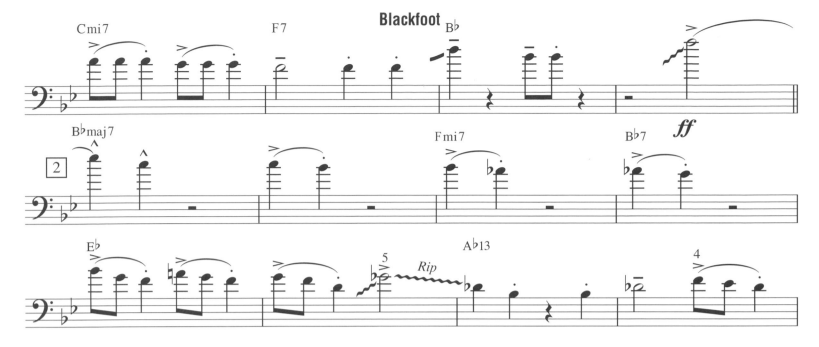

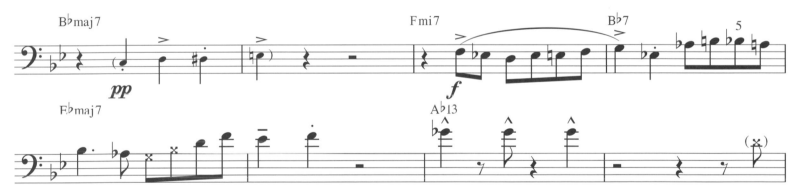

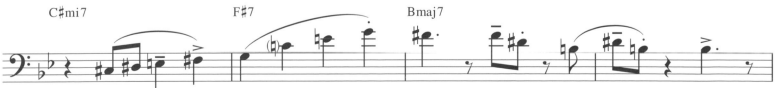

Blackfoot

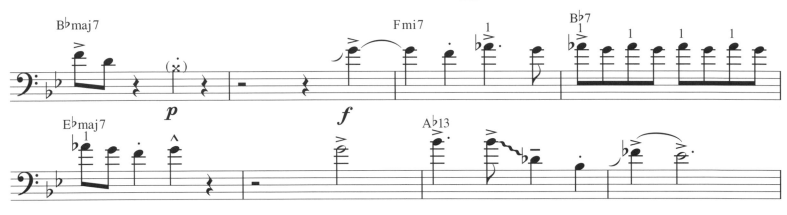

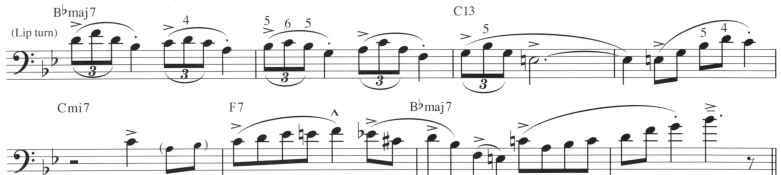

Blackfoot

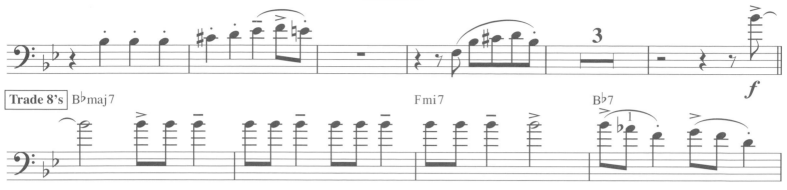

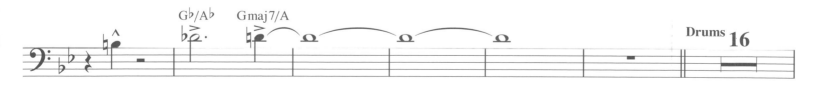

Blackfoot

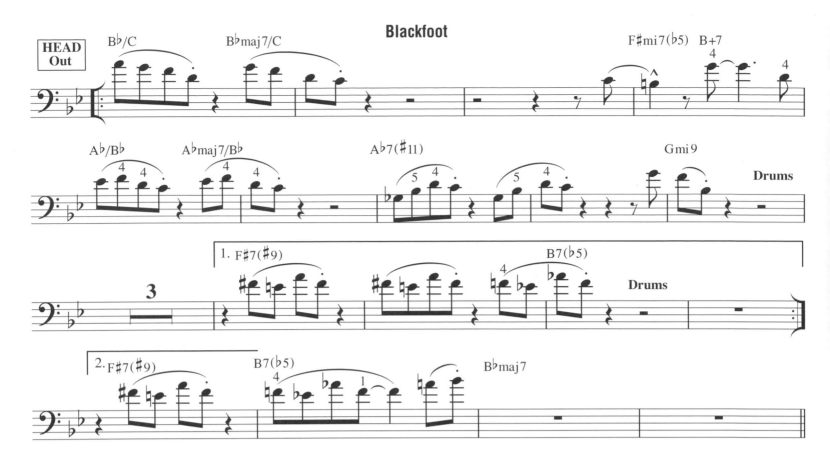

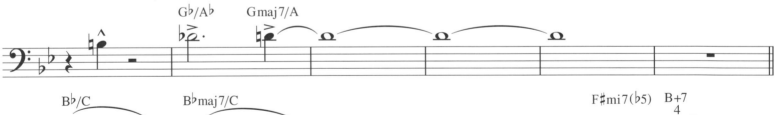

Lament

By J. J. Johnson

Trombone

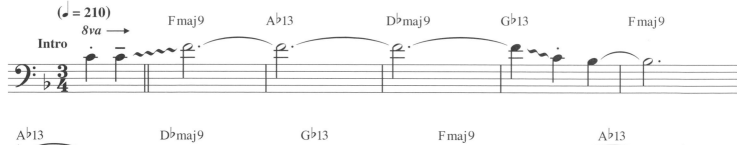

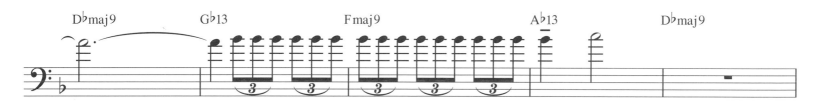

Lament

Lament

Lament

Lament

Lament

Lament

1/2 Chorus Melody and Vamp Out

Lament

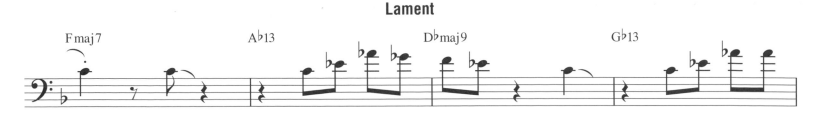

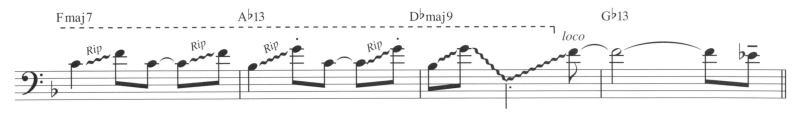

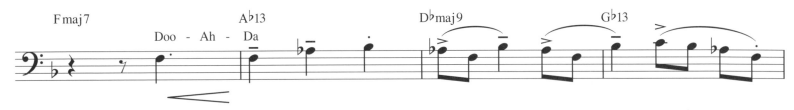

Lament

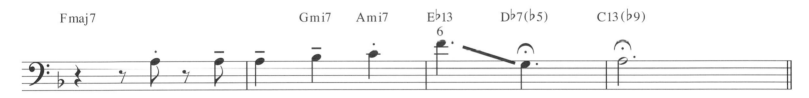

Cadenza

── **Move Slide Quickly** ──

Let It Go

By Steve Turre

Let It Go

Let It Go

Let It Go

from the Paramount Picture ROMANCE IN THE DARK

The Nearness Of You

Words by Ned Washington
Music by Hoagy Carmichael

Trombone

The Nearness Of You

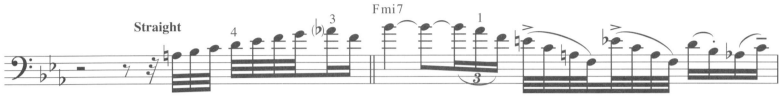

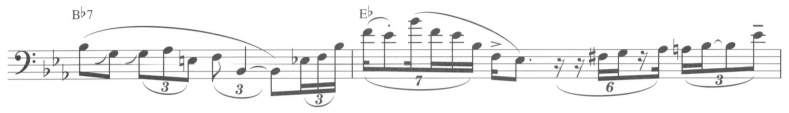

The Nearness Of You

Puente Of Soul

By Steve Turre

Trombone

Puente Of Soul

Tenor Solo

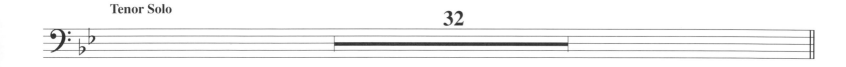

Piano Solo

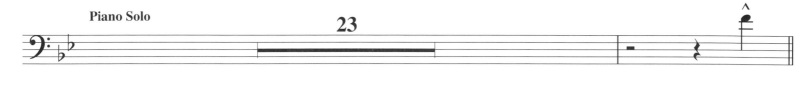

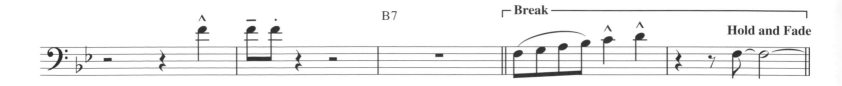

Puente Of Soul

Puente Of Soul

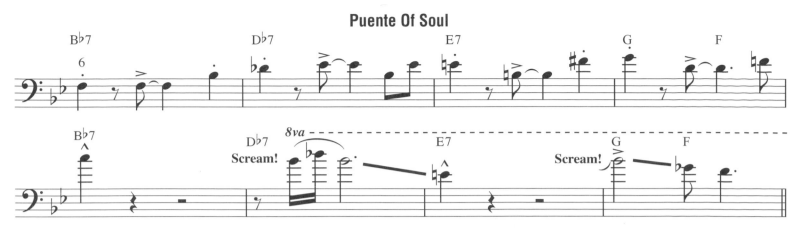

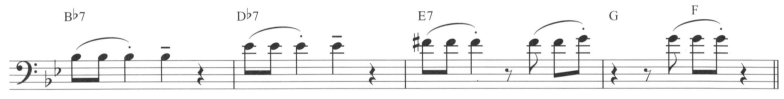

Puente Of Soul

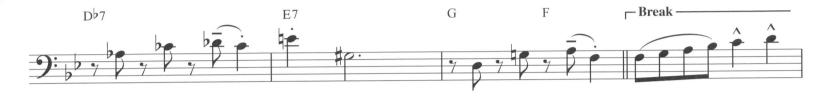

Something For John

By Steve Turre

Trombone

Something For John

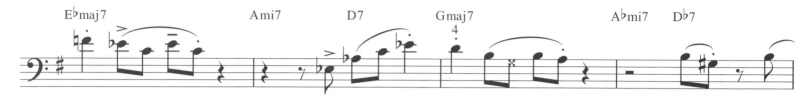

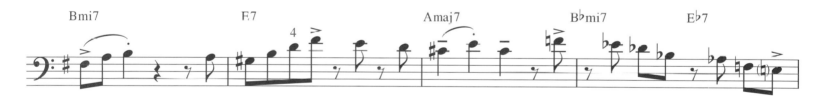

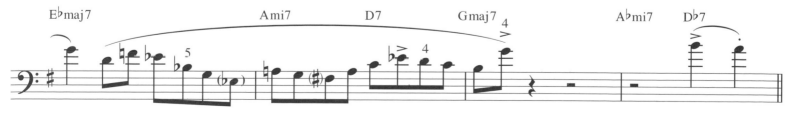

Something For John

Something For John

Something For John

Something For John

THE CUP MUTE

The cup mute, featured on "Stompin' at the Savoy," has a nice, almost "reedy" sound. It's a little softer than open horn and does not project as much, but blends well. You may have to trim the corks if you have a horn with a small bell (small bore). It's best to use sand paper so as not to take off too much at one time. Keep checking the fit as you go. It should go in the bell a good bit, but not so tight that the mute touches the bell. Leave about one half inch between the mute and the bell. If the mute is too tight, it won't "let the sound out." But if the mute is out too far, it will lose it's characteristic sound and effect.

The sound comes out of the side of the cup mute, where the mute comes close to the bell. It does not come out directly in front of the horn. Therefore, the mic placement for recording and live performance should be to the side. This will give you good sound and presence.

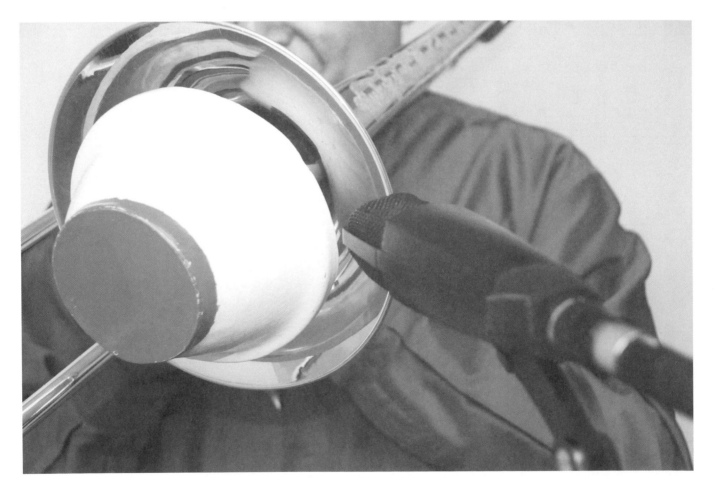

Stompin' At The Savoy

By Benny Goodman, Edgar Samson and Chick Webb

Trombone

Stompin' At The Savoy

Stompin' At The Savoy

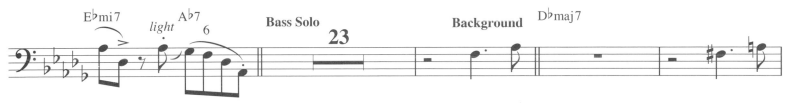

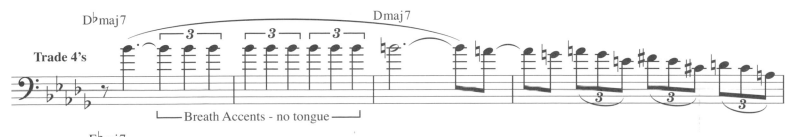

Breath Accents - no tongue

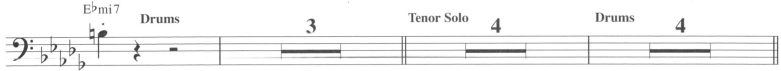

Stompin' At The Savoy

THE PLUNGER WITH PIXIE MUTE

There is more involved to playing the plunger with a pixie than just playing open horn plunger. The pixie makes it a "double mute," and you have to blow harder because there is more resistance, but the sound still can be much softer than open horn plunger. The pixie gives us the beautiful, vocal-like quality associated with Duke Ellington's music, "Tricky Sam" Nanton being the father of that sound. You can play it hard, and "holler" and "growl," or you can play it softer and get many more colors that are beautiful on ballads. You can sometimes actually say words! I learned about this from Quentin "Butter" Jackson, who played with Duke. I sat next to "Butter" in the Thad Jones / Mel Lewis Orchestra, and he explained that there is a lot more to it than just the "wha-wha" sound. There are the "oo-wha," "ah-oo," "ya-ya," and "ow-ow" sounds, and many more too!

When you first get your pixie mute, you must trim the corks so that it will fit in the bell far enough so that the plunger can close completely and seal the mute in. I suggest using sand paper rather than a knife, so you don't take off too much at one time.

The cork should taper to the small end of the mute and follow the taper of the bell. Naturally, horns with smaller bells need more sanding, but if you take off too much it won't let the sound out, and if the mute touches the bell it can "rattle" when you play. Make sure it's the correct depth in the bell.

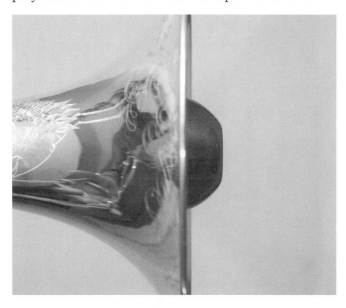

Holding the plunger is pretty simple. The thumb and little finger go on opposite outside edges, and the center of the plunger is gripped between the first and second fingers.

If this does not work for you, feel free to try something else that does, as there are no hard and fast rules. The back of the trombone (near the tuning slide) should rest on the shoulder and the front weight of the horn is shared between the hand working the slide and the hand working the plunger — like a tricycle. The bell of the trombone should rest right inside the bottom of the palm of the hand working the plunger.

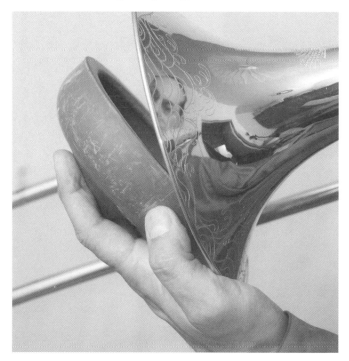

In this picture, the plunger is in half open position. The plunger is manipulated primarily with the fingers and the wrist. It takes some practice to get used to the balance and motion while holding the horn steady. Your wrist may get a little sore, because you are using new muscles. Don't worry, this will pass.

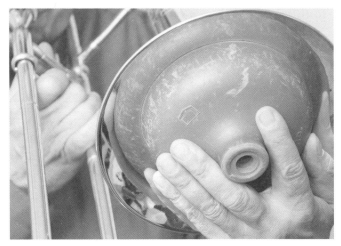

There are different positions for the plunger that give different sounds and colors. Closed position (see photo above) gives a sound like a call from the distance, or if played real loud, a buzzing sound. The "sweet spot" (see photo below) is barely open — maybe one quarter to one half inch at most. It is one of my favorites and gives the warmest, most resonant sound. It takes some practice to "find it" quickly, but let your ear guide you to the sound. The effect seems to be more dramatic and notice-able toward the upper register (F above middle C and up).

Half position (already shown on previous page) is brighter than the "sweet spot" and has a thinner sound. Open position (see photo below) is much brighter than any of the others and projects the most. I only use it occasionally, but it depends on the setting (big band vs. small group).

There is also the technique of articulating with the plunger, where you attack the note in a tight posi-tion and open the plunger quickly and in rhythm, creating an "attack" with the accompanying change of sound. This can also be done in reverse, starting from an open position and "articulating" to a closed position. Either way, it should be done in rhythm, and the plunger creates it's own "at-tack" without using the tongue. I call this "AWP" or "Articulate with Plunger," and it is notated as such in the transcriptions.

Echoes of Harlem

By Duke Ellington

Trombone

⊖ = Open a little (Sweet Spot)
AWP = Articulate with Plunger
L.V. = Lip vibrato
Trem. = Tremelo with Plunger

Echoes of Harlem

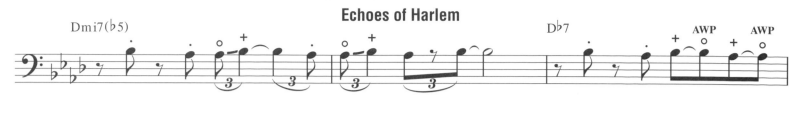

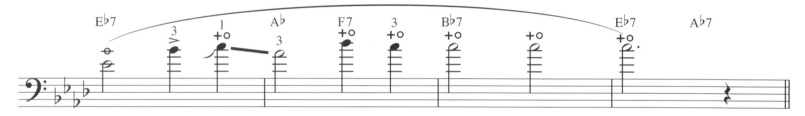

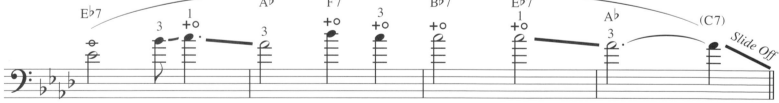

Echoes of Harlem

Head and Out

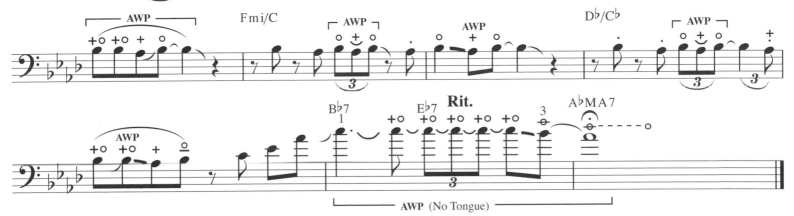

Misty

By Erroll Garner

Trombone

Misty

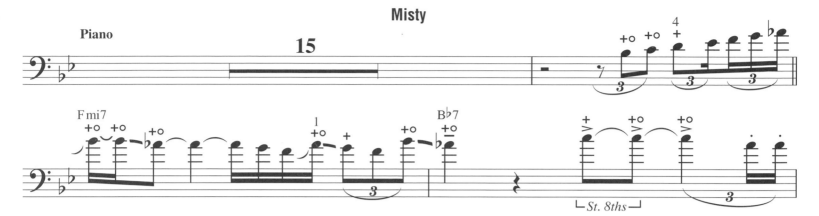

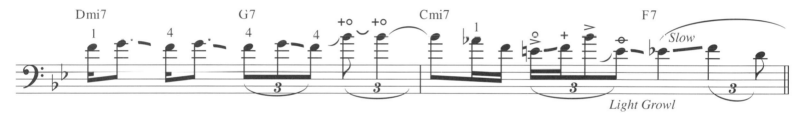

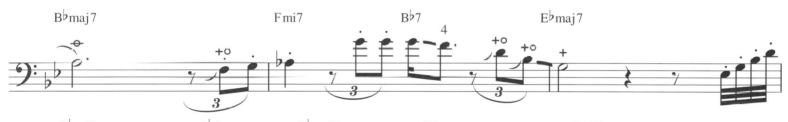

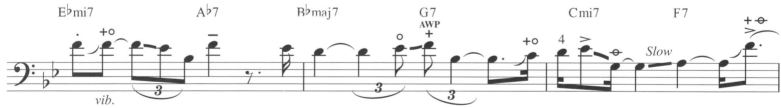

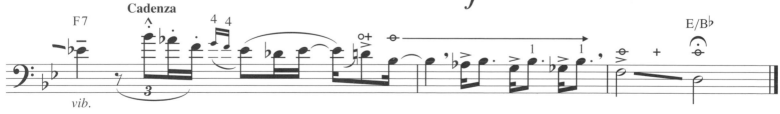

In A Sentimental Mood

By Duke Ellington

In A Sentimental Mood

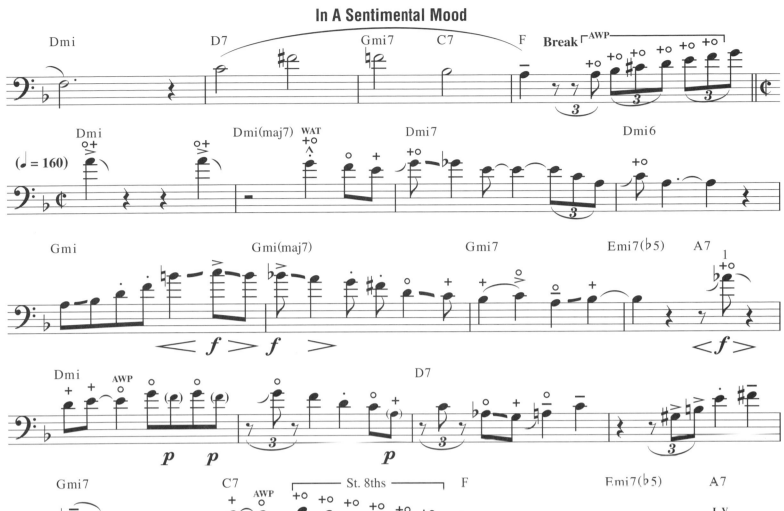

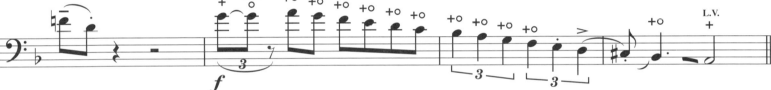

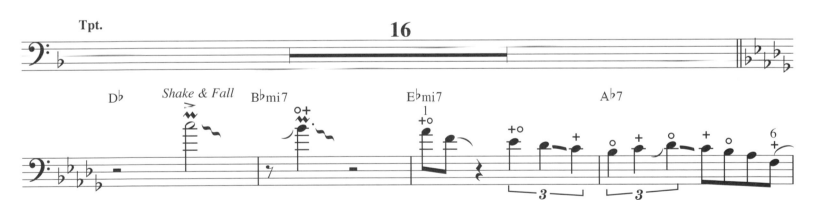

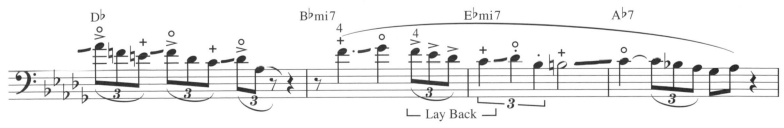

In A Sentimental Mood

from SOPHISTICATED LADIES
Mood Indigo
Trombone

Words and Music by Duke Ellington, Irving Mills and Albany Bigard

AWP = Articulate with Plunger
L.V. = Lip vibrato

Mood Indigo

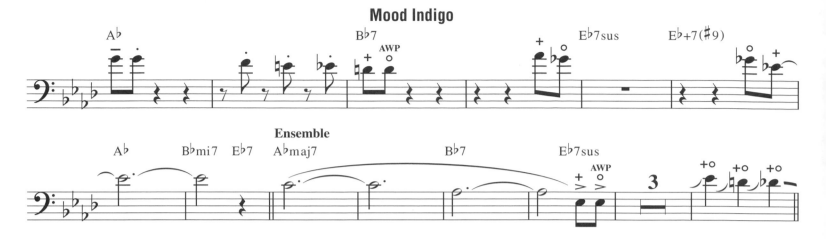

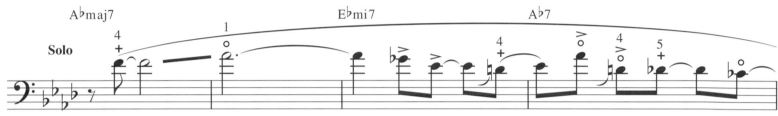

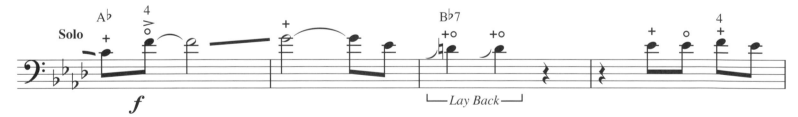

Mood Indigo

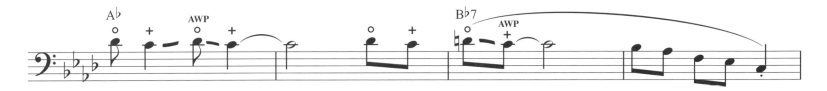

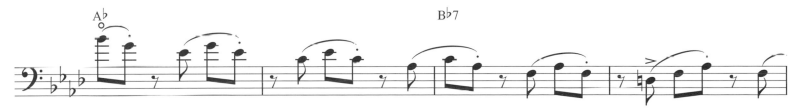

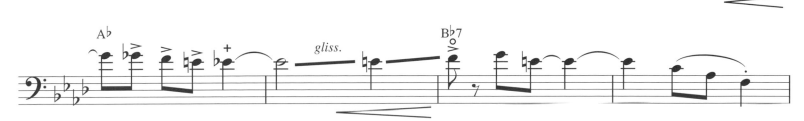

Mood Indigo

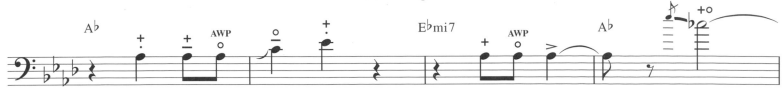

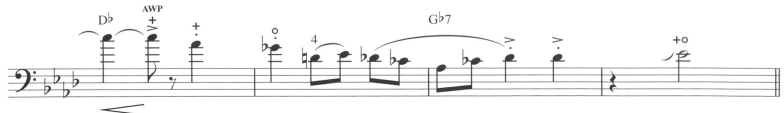

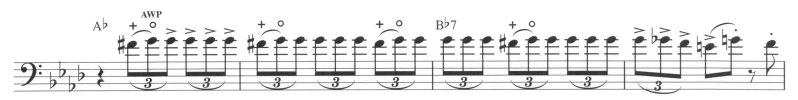

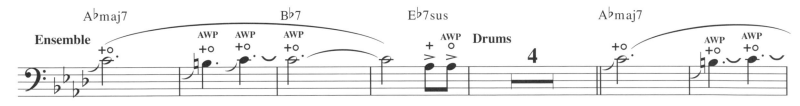

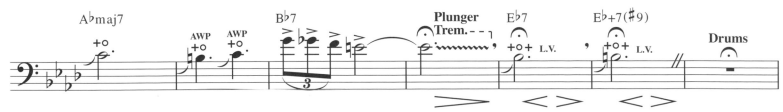

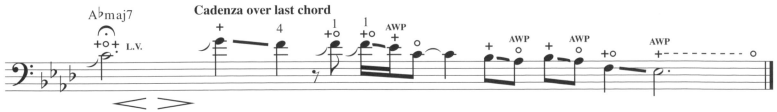

THE HARMON MUTE

I use a Harmon Mute by Joral with the stem removed. I play it on my solo in "Body and Soul." If played softly, fairly close to the mic, it gives a warm, "glassy" tone that brings to mind the hip sound Miles Davis got with a Harmon, only lower in register. I use my finger to "judge" the distance to the mic to get that sound. If you get too far from the mic, it can sound too bright. If you get to close, it can get muffled and even bang the mute into the mic unless you hold real still. Also, if you play the Harmon too loud, it gets very bright and "buzzy." This can work with the stem in when doing a "wha-wha," but it is not a mellow color. The sound comes out of the mute front and center, so the mic placement is directly in front of the bell of the trombone and mute.

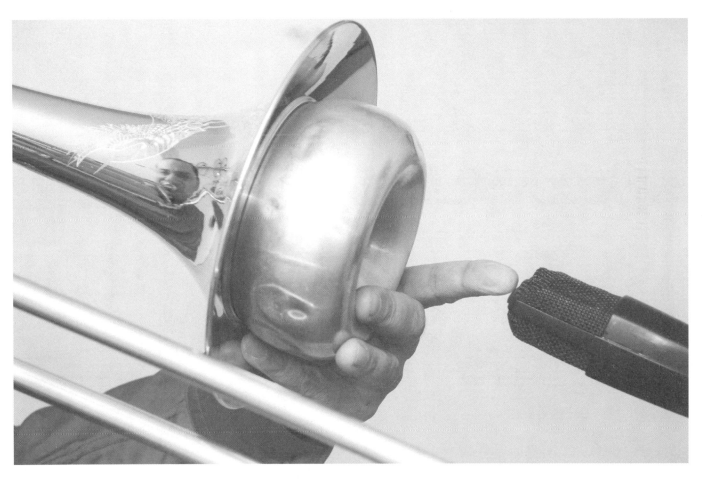

Body and Soul

Words by Edward Heyman, Robert Sour, Frank Eyton
Music by Johnny Green
Arranged by STEVE TURRE

Trombone

AWP = Articulate with Plunger
= Open a little (Sweet Spot)
L.V. = Lip vibrato

Body and Soul

Body and Soul

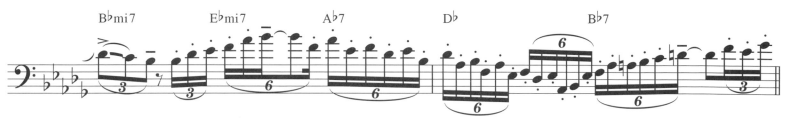

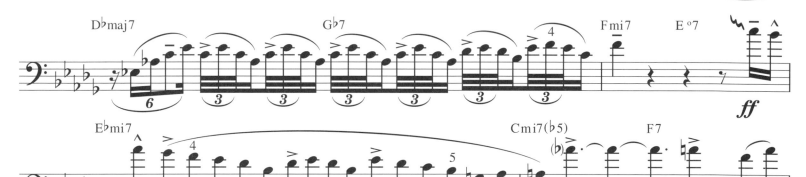

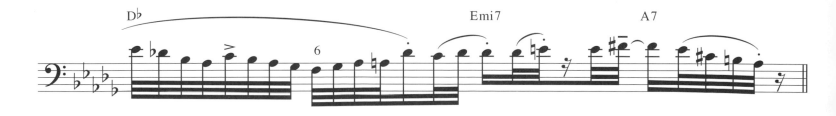

Body and Soul

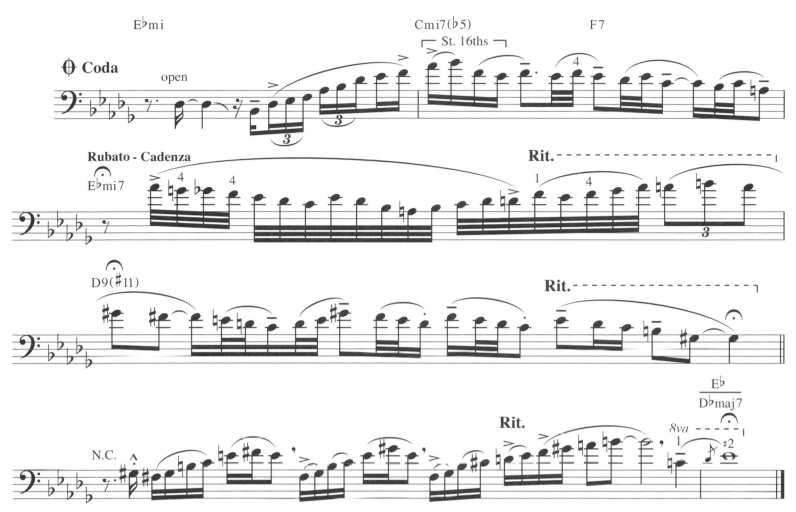

THE SEASHELL HORNS

The seashell and animal horn instruments are the roots of all brass instruments, and were played before written history. The sound is made by vibrating (buzzing) the lips. They take more air than a trombone but they have more resonance. They are totally conical by their natural design, and the sound has uncanny carrying power. Smaller shells give higher tones, and larger shells give lower pitches.

I make my own shell instruments. To make a shell horn, you must find a shell without a hole in it. (Fishermen often make holes near the tip to get the meat out.) If it has a hole, you must patch it. To make the "mouthpiece," cut off the end with a hack saw, making a hole about the size of your trombone mouthpiece. If in doubt about the correct size, it is better to make it a little small, because if you make the mouthpiece too big, you've just ruined the shell. You can always file it off a little more. After sawing the end off, you must gently tap out the center core. I use a small hammer and a screwdriver for this. Then, file it for irregularities and sand it with fine grit sand paper. If there are still inconsistencies in the rim, as is often the case, use Jet Acrylic (available at a dental supply store) and build the rim up with the plastic to an even thickness all the way around. Then, file and sand it again, and you are in business! Make sure to apply the plastic outdoors or wear a respirator that is designed for use with solvents. The fumes from the wet plastic are not healthy.

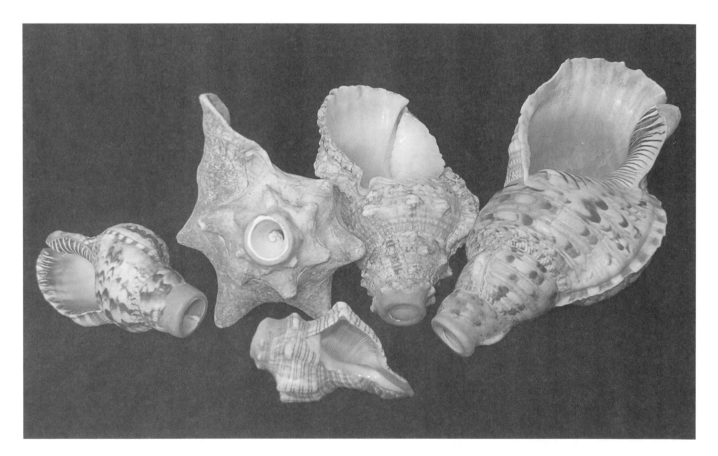

PLAYING THE SHELLS

The technique of getting different notes out of the shell is
pretty simple, and it is quite natural for trombone players!

First you must find the "primary tone." Do not
put your hand in the shell — it must be totally
open and unobstructed. The pitch produced is
the "primary tone" and is the key of your shell.

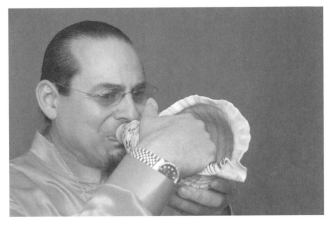

To get a whole step, put your hand in
a little more.

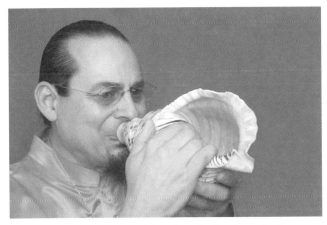

As you put your hand in the shell, the pitch goes
down, just like moving the slide of the trombone
out from first to second to third positions, etc.
To find the first half step down from the primary
tone, put your hand in just a little. Use your ear
to guide you.

You can get a third down by putting your whole
hand in, and, on some shells, you can go even
lower by putting the hand in deeper. Each
shell is different and has it's own personality.
You must spend time to learn each one as an
individual.

One of my specialties is playing two shells at
the same time to produce harmonies. I was
inspired to do this by Rahsaan Roland Kirk,
with whom I worked for many years. He
played up to three saxophones at the same
time — check it out on YouTube. When you
hear two shells on my small group records,
it is not an overdub!

Ray's Collard Greens

By Steve Turre

Trombone

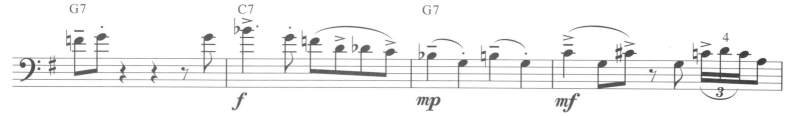

Ray's Collard Greens

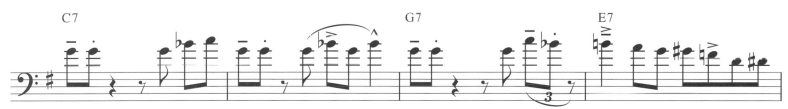

Ray's Collard Greens

Shell Solo

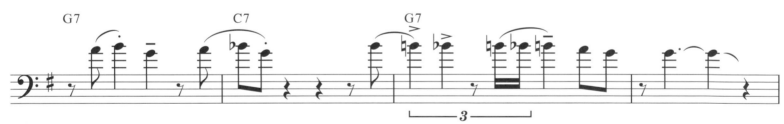

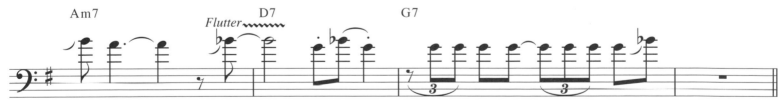

Ray's Collard Greens

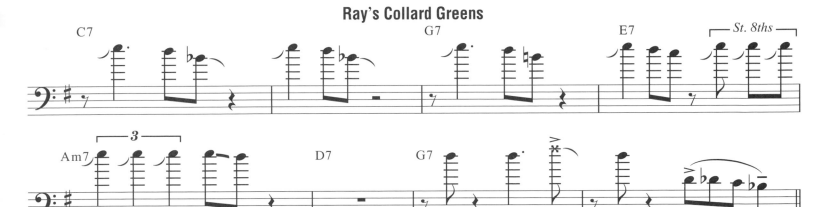

Fall with Lip

You Are The Sunshine Of My Life

Words and Music by Stevie Wonder

Trombone

Intro (♩ = 130)

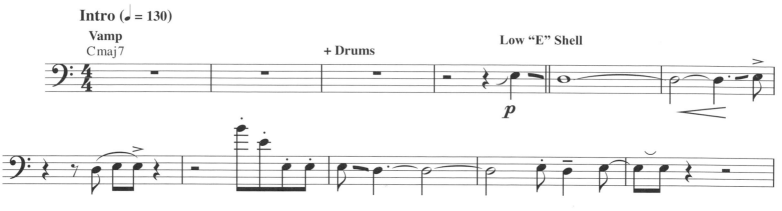

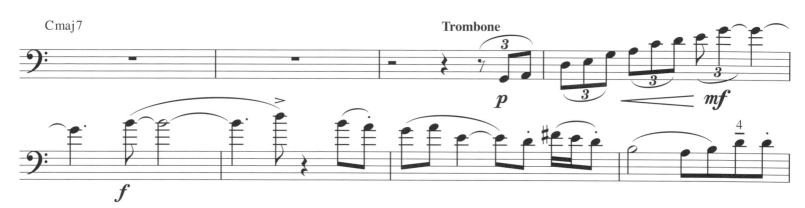

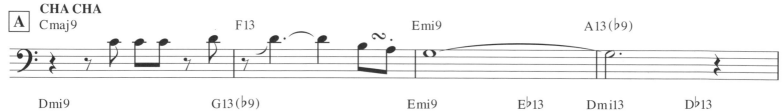

You Are The Sunshine Of My Life

You Are The Sunshine Of My Life

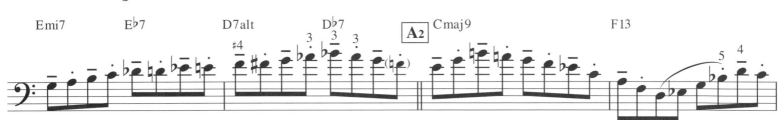

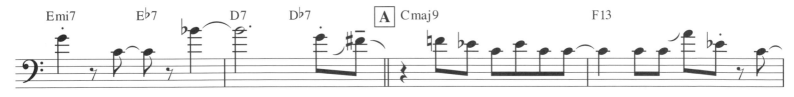

You Are The Sunshine Of My Life

You Are The Sunshine Of My Life

"E" Shell

"D" Shell

Gliss.

Vamp and Fade

Fade Out